Stardust Threads : Weaving the Self

Rahul Joshi

BookLeaf Publishing

India | USA | UK

Presentation by *BookLeaf Publishing*

Web: www.bookleafpub.com

E-mail: info@bookleafpub.com

ISBN: 9789363312364

First edition 2024

This book is dedicated to :

Everything

and, to

Everyone,

to,

The Universe,

after all,

all that exists,

is nothing but a verse of union.

PREFACE

As the author of "Stardust Threads: Weaving the Self," I stand before you, not as a distant observer of the cosmos, but as a fellow traveler on the profound journey of self-discovery. This collection of 21 poems is my humble offering to the universe—a universe that resides within each of us, vast and mysterious.

These poems are born from moments of deep reflection, from the silent conversations between the heart and the soul. They are the echoes of my innermost thoughts, the whispers of my introspective quests, and the silent screams of my existential yearnings. Each poem is a fragment of my own journey, a step towards understanding the enigma that is the self.

As you turn these pages, I hope you find solace in knowing that you are not alone in your quest. The path to self-discovery is as unique as the individual who walks it, yet there is a universal resonance in the experiences that shape us. Through these poems, I wish to connect with you, to share in the collective narrative of our human condition.

May this book serve as a compass to guide you through the landscapes of your inner world. May it be a source of comfort during times of solitude, a beacon of hope in moments of doubt, and a catalyst for transformation as you weave the self.

Welcome to "Stardust Threads: Weaving the Self." Welcome to the beginning of your odyssey.

With warmth and gratitude,
Rahul Joshi

Epiphany

In the silence of the night,
a whisper wakes the soul,
a stirring of a dream,
making the cosmos toll.

Echoes drift through the void,
a symphony of unseen light,
guiding the lost voyager,
through the shadow of the night.

Stars speak in silent riddles,
nothingness hums a tune,
to awaken the seeker,
beneath the waning moon.

Glimpses of eternity flicker,
in the corner of the eye,
secrets veiled in darkness,
as the universe softly sighs.

The world's facade falls fray,
revealing a hidden dance,
where every atom pulses,
in a cosmic trance.

Mysteries unfold their wings,
in the theatre of endless space,
inviting the mind to wander,
beyond time's relentless chase.

In the heart of the abyss,
where silence speaks so clear,
the essence of all being,
cries directly to the seer.

From this awakening,
curiosity breaks the squire,
questions after questions hurl up
as one begins to inquire.

Inquiry

Questions bloom like bubbles,
in the mind's lakeside rubbles,
whistling through pores of thought,
where answers previously sought.

Who am I, why do I exist?
To
What am I, do I even exist?
Do
I even exist,
in this vast expanse?
Do
I even exist,

amidst the cosmos' silent chant,
am I,
a spirit's curious dance?
Or am I,
a tapestry of existence,
woven just by chance.

Is that a mere glance?
My eyes in my reflection
or a divine stance
My eyes, but His projection?

Of the truth that lies hidden,
beneath the layers of self,
a treasure buried deep,
in the soul's quiet shelf,
a spark waiting to ignite,
with wisdom's wealth.
This quest for knowledge,
ever so bold,
Is a journey through the ages,
stories untold.

Learning

Pages turn, objects churn,
in the quest to know
one slowly begins to know
that to know oneself,
first all knowledge of self,
needs to die,
no room for concepts,
ideas, or frames to fly,
no images,
no reflections.
Meet the slate clean and neat,
a brand-new vessel,
filled with nothing,

made of nothing,
and only with that submission
begins, learning.

Ancient words, softly heard,
sages speak, freedom sneaks,
their voices alive,
guiding to thrive.
the fruit of truth, almost ripe,
the lime of time,
imperfect but just right,
only with discernment's eye,
and a poised gaze,
the real begins to separate
from the ephemeral haze.

Discernment

In the narrow lanes of thought,
where clowns of truth hide,
under the crayoned caricatures,
of chuckling capling jokers,
smuggling dopes of hope,
snuggling puffs of tricks and tropes,
juggling cups of evil and god,
selling dreams and gleams,
on purchase of a hidden pot.

In such dark squares and lanes,
only the guile of discernment,
can slither through
the slopes of pleasure and pain.

The guile of discernment
that echoes tales of yore,
a subtle, silent lore,
in whispers of rustling leaves,
in the wind's soft sigh,
above the narrow lanes of thought,
discernment leads to an open sky.

With eyes that see beyond the veil,
and a heart that feels the unseen,
discernment is the inner compass,
where truth has always been.
It weighs the light and shadows,
in the balance of the soul,
sifting the real from the mirage,
making the scattered—a whole.

In the moments of decision,
where paths diverge and twist,
discernment stands,
a vigilant guard, in the morning's gentle mist.

It knows the footsteps of honesty,
and the guise of deceit's charm,
holding a lantern in the night,
keeping the traveler from harm.

So listen to that silent voice,
that speaks without a word,

for truth is not in meaning and order,
it's in the chaos and the absurd,
meaning and order bring attachment,
but to fly freely under the sky,
one must first learn detachment.

Detachment

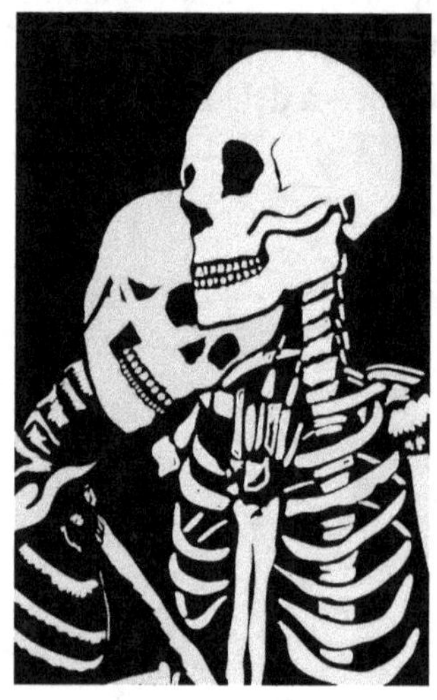

In the quiet of the twilight,
where the stars begin to gleam,
lies the realm of sweet detachment,
like a softly whispered dream,
where the heart unbinds its fetters,
and the mind is free to roam,
in the silence of the spaces,
where the soul finds peace, its home.

No more clinging to the shadows,
no more grasping for the light,
just the tranquil sense of being,
in the calmness of the night.

Like a leaf that's gently falling,
from the tree to the earth below,
embracing change with grace,
allowing life's true colors to show.

Detachment is not uncaring,
it's the wisdom of the sage,
who sees the world's vast scenery,
from outside the gilded cage.

It is the dance of liberation,
from the chains we thought were dear,
finding strength within the stillness,
letting go of every fear.
With virtue as the vessel,
the journey takes its course,
guided by the stars,
with inner light as the source.

Virtue

With every deed in grace,
and every thought pure,
the path becomes clear,
the journey sure.
A step taken in kindness,
a word spoken in love,
a contagious smile,
a youthful guile,
lifts the heart higher,
to the realms above.

In the practice of virtue,
the soul's light shines,
guiding the way forward,

through the pines.
The mind now ready,
for stillness to embrace,
finds its solace,
in meditation's grace.

Meditation

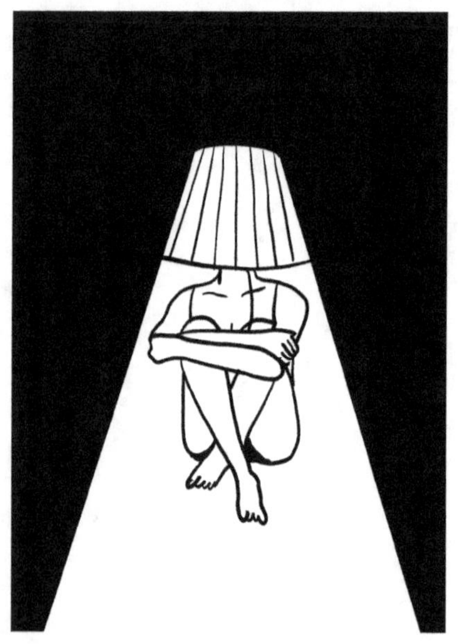

A whisper in the silence,
a hush in the inward isle,
pick breath as your guide,
with stillness, stretched for a Nile.

Gaze, not as a sage so wise.
Gaze, as a child, with open eyes.
In the lap of vast serenity,
meet with the heart's pure entity.

The world outside spins and roars,
the calm inside acts as an oar,
to row across the inner seas,
through tides of turmoil,
to ultimate inner peace.

Step by step, with each breath,
dive into the deep,
where secrets of the soul sleep,
wander through the inner caves,
beyond the mind's relentless waves.

Heart beats to a rhythmic chant,
a sacred dance, a holy plant,
form the seeds of quietude,
in the lap of meditation's solitude.

No longer just a practice, but a living art,
where ending becomes the start,
and with concentration's power,
the inner flame begins to flower,
a journey deep into the vast,
where the self is to be found at last.

Concentration

A focused flame,
unwavering and bright,
sets of silhouettes,
banished throughout the night.

Like a spider,
weaving webs with care,
each thread, a line of focus,
spun through the air.
Or like a cat,
eyes fixed upon a fluttering hare,
embodying a focused flare.

Concentration,
a painter with a single hue,
finding depth in simplicity,
as masters do.
A sculptor,
chiseling away the stone's excess,
revealing forms of beauty
and finesse.

Now picture a juggler,
with balls in the sky,
keeping them aloft,
as time ticks by.
A delicate balance,
a dance of the mind,
where each thought is caught
and then aligned.

In the silence of space,
where stars are born,
and where the poem finds its final line,
concentration leads to the divine.
In the stillness, where all is free,
rests the tranquil sea of tranquility.

Tranquility

Beneath the canopy of turmoil and plight,
where moths of perception often take flight,
lies a meadow, vast and wide,
a canvas for the stars to confide.

No echoes of the day's loud roar,
just the ocean's distant shore,
whispering secrets, old as time,
in rhythm, reason and rhyme.

A fox trotting softly through the dew,
its coat—a brushstroke against the hue,
painting paths that twist and wind,
in the gallery of a tranquil mind.

Fireflies dance in the cool air,
a symphony of sparks, fair and rare,
each a thought, bright and brief,
in the quietude of evaporating belief.

And there, in the heart of the serene,
a single lotus blooms unseen,
rooted deep in the silent firth,
a testament to the tranquil earth.

As dawn approaches, shy and slight,
the meadow fades into the light,
and then the lotus in its quietest berth,
whispers insight of immeasurable worth.

Insight

A flash of the divine,
a celestial spark;
Ignites the chambers
of the heart,
not a mere flicker,
but a cosmic confluence,
where time dissolves,
and existence finds resonance.

In the mind's quiet land,
where thoughts tiptoe,
the noise of the world fades,
like echoes in a cave,
and there, in the stillness,
the universe shivers and misbehaves.

Revealing the unseen,
threads of stardust spun,
connecting galaxies, souls,
and the rising sun.
Each thread a story,
etched in cosmic ink,
of birth, death, love,
and how the galaxies think.

Woven by a cosmic hand,
ancient and wise,
the warp and weft of existence,
a grand enterprise.
Planets pirouette,
comets compose their trails,
and quasars hum secrets,
like ancient bards' tales.

In the moment of insight,
the veil lifts,
not just from the eyes,
but from the soul's rifts.
The seeker glimpses eternity,
a timeless dance,
where past, present, and future
intertwine and enhance.

A story of oneness,
whispered by the wind,

of atoms and galaxies,
of beginnings and no end,
heart expands, supernovas bloom,
as they touch the hem
of truth in the quiet room.

The ego surrenders,
a fragile paper boat,
floating on the river of existence,
without a moat,
no longer the captain,
but a passenger of grace,
in the light of insight,
all find their place.

Surrender

Ego falls like autumn leaves,
upon the ground,
in surrender's embrace,
the self is unbound.

Walls of resistance crumble,
the barriers fade,
in the act of surrender,
the foundation is laid.

For a temple of openness,
where the divine resides,

in the heart of the seeker,
where truth abides.

In the silence of letting go,
a whisper is heard,
the call of the infinite,
beyond the word.

In the space of nothingness,
a new self emerges,
purified by surrender,
as the spirit converges.

With each breath released,
a new one taken,
in the cycle of surrender,
the old is forsaken.

In the depths of surrender,
the ego dissolves,
and in its place, a unity,
around which everything resolves.

For in the act of giving in,
we truly receive,
the essence of existence,
the soul's reprieve.

So let go and fall,
like the leaf to the earth,
for in surrender's hold,
we find our rebirth.

Through grace,
the journey is blessed,
leading to transformation,
where the soul finds rest.

Grace

Blessings flow,
like Ganga to the sea,
in grace's gentle touch,
the soul flies free.
Unseen hands guide,
the path becomes clear,
in the warmth of grace,
there's nothing to fear.

The seeker's journey,
now touched by the divine,
moves forward with ease,
like a sacred sign.
The old self peels away,
layer by layer,

revealing the true self,
rarer and fairer.

With grace as the guide,
the spirit soars high,
beyond the reach of troubles,
under the vast sky.
Each step is lighter,
as burdens release,
in the dance of grace,
all discord will cease.

The heart sings a melody,
pure and sincere,
In harmony with grace,
love draws near.
The tapestry of life,
now vivid and bright,
is woven with threads of grace,
in the loom of light.

In the mirror of grace,
reflections shine true,
showing a vision of life,
in a radiant hue.
The soul, once entangled,
now gracefully weaves,
a story of transformation,
like the fresh new leaves.

Transformation

From the cocoon emerges,
not what once was,
but a being of light,
abiding by cosmic laws..

In the flames of transformation,
the true self is born,
radiant and free,
like the light of dawn,
with perseverance's might,
the seeker stands tall,
ready to face any storm,
ready to answer the call.

Through the silence of introspection,
the spirit takes flight,
ascending to heights,
untouched by the night,
the heart's quiet whisper
becomes a guiding song,
leading the way,
where the brave belong.

In the garden of change,
where the soul finds its wings,
the dance of evolution,
a sacred thing.
Each step, a testament
to the strength within,
a journey of growth,
a rebirth to begin.

The mirror reflects
a story untold,
of a phoenix rising,
bold and bold.
No longer bound
by the chains of the past,
embracing a future,
vast and vast.

So let the winds of change blow,
unfurling the sail,
set course on a voyage
where the brave prevail.
For, in the quest of transformation,
one finds their truth,
a timeless odyssey,
in the fountain of youth.
With perseverance's might,
the seeker stands tall,
ready to face any storm,
ready to answer the call.

Perseverance

Through storms and trials,
no swaying away,
for in perseverance's fire,
the night turns to day.
Step by step,
the mountain is climbed,
with each breath taken,
the spirit is primed.

In the heart's quiet whisper,
the purpose is found,

the journey is not lonely,
for hope is a guide,
in the dance of the cosmos,
we are the stars that collide.

With courage as compass,
the path is made clear,
through forests of doubt,
we conquer fear.
The summit in sight,
horizons expand,
in the grasp of our hands,
the universe is grand.

So let the storms come,
let the trials commence,
our spirits, unbroken,
will stand in defense.
for we are the seekers,
in life's grand play,
and in perseverance's fire,
we forge our way.

The wisdom gained,
now part of the soul,
leads to integration,
making the seeker—a whole.

Integration

In the quiet of the cosmos,
where whispers roam,
a longing stirs
within the heart's dome.
For the unity of all,
a yearning so deep,
a desire for connection,
too profound to keep.

A dissolving gaze
at the vast night sky,
A silent plea
in the soul's soft sigh.
An ache for the stars,
for the infinite space,
to be one with the universe,
in its graceful embrace.

The dance of life,
a wistful tune,
under the watchful eye
of the crescent moon.
The seeker's heart,
in a tender braid,
with the fabric of existence,
intricately laid.

This longing,
a beacon in the endless night,
guiding the spirit
to merge with the light.
A thirst for the whole,
for the boundless divine,
in the integration of self,
all is aligned.

The universe responds,
a gentle caress,

a promise of union,
in the cosmic expanse,
in the dance of life,
the heart's eternal chance.

Non-duality

No 'I' or 'you',
just an endless sea,
a red hot blue,
where waves of beings,
whisper 'we are thee.'
The illusion of separation,
melts away,
electron is electricity,
night is the same as day,
player is the play,

thinker of this thought,
converts the seeker into sought,
a strange union, stirs bliss,
tears of joy, flow like a silent hiss.

Bliss

Light dances on leaves,
plays peek-a-boo
under the trees,
air hums with peace,
the burdens of life,
for a moment, cease.
Heart sings in chorus
with the sky above,
in the garden of joy,
cradled in love.

Petals unfurl,
a magic show appears,
Apples papples
papples pears
eyes spies
bubbles bears
noses roses
dozes poses
meaning loses
logic loses
knowledge loses
loses all that might
and will
only an intense bliss prevails
it all makes sense
chaos makes sense
garden of joy;
a forest so dense.

After the laughter,
complete silence takes over,
it takes you from you
and keeps it in front of you
and when you look at you
with all new
point of view
happiness and silence
merge into one
a skin of infinity
peeled off from unity.

Silence

.... ;

...... ,

..............;

..........,

...

..

.

....;

....,

............;

....,

...,

..

.

Unity

All life entwined,
everything glitters divine,
the self reflects
in every face,
life emerges
in every place.

The knots of life,
unites multiple threads,
in every hue and form,
not-two spreads,
from the same sacred source,
all that exists arrive,

into the same sacred source,
all that exists will ultimately dive.

Boundaries blur,
the distinctions fade,
in the light of one sun,
the world gets remade,
a music of souls,
a harmonious stroll,

Embraced in this union,
a light of lightness exists,
a new sense of freedom
a new set of wings.

Freedom

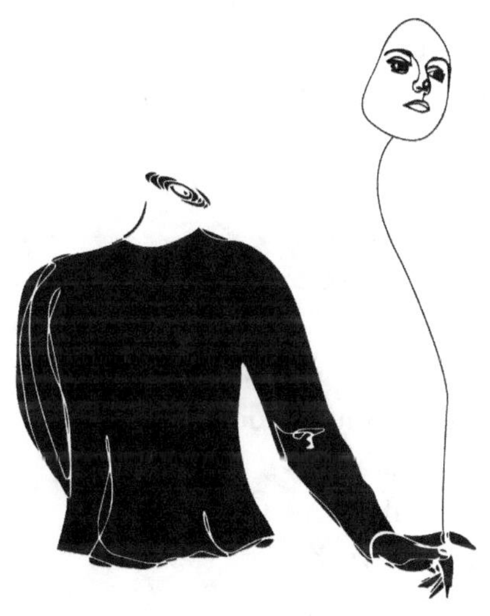

Birth and death,
the two events merge,
in freedom's vast expanse,
all time and space converge.
Free from the cycle,
that binds and ties,
past, present and future,
in a moment
it all flies.

The mind,
uncluttered by the past,
sees the now,

sees what is,
no reflections from thought,
no projection from the known,
in freedom's field,
the seeds of realization are sown.

Liberation from the me,
leaves the self behind,
with nothing as separate,
one is truly free.
On this boundless meadow,
where ego casts no shadow,
the light of truth,
clear and bright,
makes the self visible
in pure sight.

Realization

In the silent laughter of the universe,
giggles of life disperse,
one finds in the vast expanse,
the simple truth of life's dance.

The journey, a play of light and shade,
a spectacle very well played,
the self, a witness to the grand show,
in realization's light, begins to know,
that there was nothing to be found,
all that there was;
just reverberations of a sound.

A sound of laughter,
that the universe emanates.
A cosmic joke,
the universe perpetuates.
It echoes in the blackened void,

in every asteroid deployed,
in every planet's spin and twirl,
a silent chuckle, a subtle swirl.

It's in the joy of a star's light,
that travels through the endless night,
to greet your eyes from ages past,
in silent laughter, endless and vast.

The game of life, a dream within,
a spectacle of sound, a vibrant din.
Yet in the silence, wisdom's key,
unlocks the door to what is free.

"I am That"—the ultimate decree.
In realization's dawn, the self is the sea.
That art Thou or TaT Tvam Asi!